CW01096061

FSMQ
in a Nutshell

ADDITIONAL MATHEMATICS
OCR SYLLABUS

THE MATHS CLINIC

ISBN-10:1543185266
ISBN-13:978-1543185263

DEDICATED TO THE SERIOUS STUDENT

"The building blocks of understanding are memorisation and repetition"

-Barbara Oakley-

CONTENTS

THE Q&A WAY   7

Q&A IN ALGEBRA   8

Q&A IN BINOMIAL EXPANSION   25

Q&A IN COORDINATE GEOMETRY   29

Q&A IN LINEAR PROGRAMMING   36

Q&A IN TRIGONOMETRY   43

Q&A IN 3D TRIG PROBLEMS   58

Q&A IN CALCULUS   61

Q&A IN KINEMATICS   73

RAPID REVISION QUIZ   79

THE Q&A WAY

Drawing from years of teaching Mathematics, The Maths Clinic has devised a foolproof method to master mathematical concepts for success in exams.

Armed with pen and notepad, follow the Q&A way as you revise and learn all you need to know for FSMQ – the Additional Mathematics examination.

The FSMQ syllabus covers the four main branches of Pure Mathematics – Algebra, Co-ordinate Geometry, Trigonometry and Calculus and introduces with each branch a topic of Applied Mathematics.

The book is divided into three sections – Questions, Answers and a Rapid Revision Quiz.
The **Question section** breaks up the entire syllabus into a mixture of questions on key facts, formulae, working steps, derivations and problems.

The **Answer section** states the key facts, formulae, working steps, derivations and provides working solutions to all problems.

The **Rapid Revision Quiz section** lists out only the questions that test your knowledge of all the topics.. Quiz questions appear in bold print in each Question section.

We recommend a thorough exam preparation to include the following:
Step 1:
Work through all the questions diligently– memorising facts and practising problems.
Step 2:
Test yourself several times with the Rapid Revision Quiz section. Create a batch of record cards and practise with them. The mastery of the Quiz questions will lead to the mastery of the knowledge base required for FSMQ.
Step 3:
Answer at least five past exam question papers completely and within the prescribed time.

Q&A IN ALGEBRA

1. FACTORISATION
   a. **State the three methods of factorisation.**
   b. Factorise: $2xy^2 - 12x^2y =$
   c. Factorise: $1 - \frac{9}{49}x^2 =$
   d. Factorise: $x^2 + 8x + 15 =$
   e. Factorise: $2x^2 - 11x - 21 =$
   f. **Difference of 2 squares: $x^2 - y^2 =$**

2. CHANGE OF SUBJECT OF FORMULA
   a. **State the rules for change of subject of formula.**
   b. Make a the subject of the formula $s = ut + \frac{1}{2}at^2$
   c. Make h the subject of the formula $D = \sqrt{2Rh}$

3. QUADRATIC EQUATIONS
   a. **List three methods for solving quadratic equations.**
   b. Solve: $2x^2 - 3x - 27 = 0$
   c. **Completing the square formula: $x^2 + bx =$**
   d. Solve by completing the square and give the answer correct to 2 decimal places: $3x^2 + 6x + 2 = 0$
   e. **Quadratic formula: $x =$**
   f. Solve by using the quadratic formula and give the answer correct to 2 decimal places: $x^2 - x - 8 = 0$

4. EXPANSION - 1
   a. **Describe FOIL expansion for multiplying expressions.**
   b. Expand using FOIL $(2x + 3)(3x - 5) =$

5. EXPANSION - 2
   a. **Expansion: $(x + y)(x - y) =$**
   b. Expand: : $(7a + 5b)(7a - 5b) =$

6.   EXPANSION - 3
   a.   **Expansion:** $(x + y)^2 =$
   b.   Expand: $(3x + \frac{1}{3})^2 =$

7.   EXPANSION - 4
   a.   **Expansion:** $(x - y)^2 =$
   b.   Expand: : $(1 - 2n)^2$

8.   COMPLETING THE SQUARE
   a.   Find the values of a and b where
        $x^2 + 8x = (x + a)^2 + b$
   b.   **Given a curve $y = ax^2 + bx + c$, state the line of symmetry.**
   c.   State the line of symmetry for the curve
        $y = 4x^2 + 4x - 15$
   d.   **Given a curve $y = ax^2 + bx + c$, state the coordinates of the vertex or the turning point.**
   e.   State the coordinates of the vertex of the curve
        $y = 2x^2 - 3x - 27$.
   f.   **Given a curve $y = ax^2 + bx + c$, what is the y-intercept?**
   g.   What is the y-intercept for the curve $y = 9x^2 - 30x + 25$?
   h.   **Given that the coordinates of the turning point of a quadratic graph are (a, b) then the quadratic equation is given by:_____.**
   i.   Given the coordinates of the turning point of a quadratic graph are $(-1, 5)$, state the quadratic equation.

9. SIMULTANEOUS EQUATIONS
   a. Solve linear and quadratic equations:
   $$x^2 + y^2 = 20$$
   $$y - x = 6$$

   b. Solve simultaneous equations:
   $$4x + 5y = 14$$
   $$8x - 3y = 2$$

10. LINEAR INEQUALITIES
    Solve and represent solutions on the number line.
    a. $5 + 3x \geq 11$
    b. $4 \leq 5x - 6 < 14$
    c. $5 > 9 - 4x > 1$

11. QUADRATIC INEQUALITIES
    a. **State the steps to solving a quadratic inequality**.
    b. $3x^2 + 2x - 1 > 0$
    c. $x^2 - 5x + 6 < 0$
    d. $8 - 2x \geq x^2$

12. ALGEBRAIC FRACTIONS
    a. Simplify $\frac{x^2-4x+4}{x^2-2x} \div \frac{x^2-4}{x-2}$
    b. Solve for x: $\frac{2}{3x-1} + \frac{1}{x+8} = \frac{1}{2}$

13. SURDS
    a. **Define a surd.**
    b. Simplify the following: $2\sqrt{125} - 3\sqrt{20}$
    c. **What are the 3 rules of surds?**
    d. Rationalise $\frac{15}{\sqrt{5}}$
    e. Simplify: $\left(3 + \sqrt{2}\right)\left(5 - 2\sqrt{2}\right) =$

14. FACTOR THEOREM
    a. **Define the order of a polynomial.**
    b. Divide $(x^3 + 2x^2 - x - 2)$ by $(x - 1)$
    c. **State the factor theorem.**
    d. Factorise the following function $2x^3 + 7x^2 + 7x + 2$ as a product of 3 linear factors.
    e. Given that $f(x) = x^3 + 3x^2 - x - 3$,
        ii   Show that $(x + 1)$ is a factor of $f(x)$
        iii Factorise . $f(x)$
        iiii Solve $f(x) = 0$

15. REMAINDER THEOREM
    a. **State the remainder theorem.**
    b. Find the remainder when $x^3 - 3x^2 + 5x + 10$ is divided by $(x - 4)$.
    c. When $x^3 + 4x^2 + ax + 6$ is divided by $(x + 5)$, the remainder is -4. What is a?

1. FACTORISATION
   a. State the three methods of factorisation.
      1. Take out common factors
      2. Difference of 2 squares
      3. Cross Method

   b. Factorise: $2xy^2 - 12x^2y$
      Take out common factors
      $2xy^2 - 12x^2y$
      $= 2xy(y - 6x)$

   c. Factorise: $1 - \frac{9}{49}x^2$
      Difference of 2 squares
      $1 - \frac{9}{49}x^2$
      $= (1 + \frac{3}{7}x)(1 - \frac{3}{7}x)$

   d. Factorise: $x^2 + 8x + 15$
      Cross Method: (Coefficient of x^2 is 1)

      Find factors of 15 that when multiplied along the diagonals add to give 8x.

      x $+3$
      x $+5$

      $x^2 + 8x + 15 = (x + 3)(x + 8)$

   e. Factorise: $3x^2 + 11x + 6$
      Cross Method: (Coefficient of x^2 is not 1)

      x $+2$
      x $+9$

      Factorise: $3x^2 + 11x \oplus 6$
      Factors of $3 \times 6 = 18$
      $= 2 \times 9$ that add to give $+11x$
      Multiply along diagonals to
      give $2x + 9x = +11x$

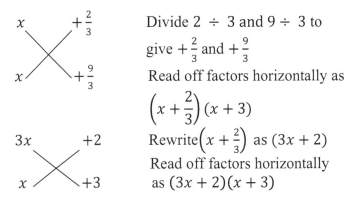

Divide $2 \div 3$ and $9 \div 3$ to

give $+\frac{2}{3}$ and $+\frac{9}{3}$

Read off factors horizontally as

$\left(x + \frac{2}{3}\right)(x + 3)$

Rewrite $\left(x + \frac{2}{3}\right)$ as $(3x + 2)$

Read off factors horizontally

as $(3x + 2)(x + 3)$

f.   Difference of 2 squares: $x^2 - y^2 = (x + y)(x - y)$

2.   CHANGE OF SUBJECT OF FORMULA
   a.   State the rules for change of subject of formula.
       Rules for change of subject of formula:
       i.   Swap sides to get the required subject on the
            left hand side (LHS) of the equals sign.
       ii.   Start moving non-subject variables from the
            LHS of the equals sign to the right hand side
            (RHS) by reversing each operation.
       iii.   Addition$\Leftrightarrow$Subtraction
            Multiplication$\Leftrightarrow$Division
            Square$\Leftrightarrow$Square root
            Cube$\Leftrightarrow$Cube root
   b.   Make a the subject of the formula $s = ut + \frac{1}{2}at^2$
       Swap sides

$$ut + \frac{1}{2}at^2 = s$$

$$\frac{1}{2}at^2 = s - ut$$

$$\therefore a = \frac{2(s - ut)}{t^2}$$

c. Make h the subject of the formula $D = \sqrt{2Rh}$
    Swap sides
    $\sqrt{2Rh} = D$
    Squaring both sides
    $2Rh = D^2$
    $\therefore h = \dfrac{D^2}{2R}$

3. QUADRATIC EQUATIONS
    a. Three methods for solving quadratic equations are by:
        1. Factorisation
        2. Completing the square
        3. Quadratic formula
    b. Solve: $2x^2 - 3x - 27 = 0$
        By factorising using Cross Method, we have

2x   − 9

x   + 3

        Factors of -54 that differ by -3 are -9 and $+6$
        Divide each factor by 2
        $\left(x - \dfrac{9}{2}\right)\left(x + \dfrac{6}{2}\right) = 0$
        $\therefore x = \dfrac{9}{2}, x = -3$

    c. Completing the square formula:
        $x^2 + bx = \left(x + \dfrac{b}{2}\right)^2 - \left(\dfrac{b}{2}\right)^2$
    d. Solve by completing the square and give the answer correct to 2 decimal places: $3x^2 + 6x + 2 = 0$
        $3(x^2 + 2x) + 2 = 0$
        $3(x^2 + 2x) = -2$
        $3[(x + 1)^2 - 1] = -2$
        $3(x + 1)^2 - 3 = -2$
        $3(x + 1)^2 = 1$
        $(x + 1)^2 = \dfrac{1}{3}$

$$x + 1 = \pm \frac{1}{\sqrt{3}}$$

$$x = -1 \pm \frac{1}{\sqrt{3}} = -0.42, -1.58$$

e. Quadratic formula:
$$x = \frac{-b \pm \sqrt{b^2 - 4ac}}{2a}$$

f. Solve by using the quadratic formula and give the answer correct to 2 decimal places: $x^2 - x - 8 = 0$
$$a = 1, b = -1, c = -8$$
$$x = \frac{1 \pm \sqrt{1 - 4(1)(-8)}}{2}$$
$$x = \frac{1 \pm \sqrt{33}}{2} = 3.37, -2.37$$

4. EXPANSION - 1
    a. Describe FOIL expansion for multiplying two binomial expressions.
        FOIL: Multiply (First, Outer, Inner, Last) terms.

    b. Expand using FOIL
        $(2x + 3)(3x - 5)$
        $= 6x^2 - 10x + 9x - 15$
        $= 6x^2 - x - 15$

5. EXPANSION - 2
    a. Expansion: $(x + y)(x - y) = x^2 - y^2$
    b. Expand: : $(7a + 5b)(7a - 5b) = 49a^2 - 25b^2$

6. EXPANSION - 3
    a. Expansion: $(x + y)^2 = x^2 + 2xy + y^2$
    b. Expand: : $\left(3x + \frac{1}{3}\right)^2$
        $= 9x^2 + 2(3x)\left(\frac{1}{3}\right) + \left(\frac{1}{3}\right)^2$
        $= 9x^2 + 2x + \frac{1}{9}$

7. **EXPANSION - 4**
   a. Expansion: $(x - y)^2 = x^2 - 2xy + y^2$
   b. Expand: $(1 - 2n)^2$
   $$= 1 - 2(1)(2n) + 4n^2$$
   $$= 1 - 4n + 4n^2$$

8. **COMPLETING THE SQUARE**
   a. Find the values of a and b where
   $$x^2 + 8x = (x + a)^2 + b$$
   $$x^2 + 8x = (x + 4)^2 - 16$$
   b. Given a curve $y = ax^2 + bx + c$, state the line of symmetry.
   Line of symmetry is: $x = \dfrac{-b}{2a}$
   c. State the line of symmetry for the curve
   $$y = 4x^2 + 4x - 15$$
   Line of symmetry is: $x = \dfrac{-b}{2a}$
   $: x = \dfrac{-(4)}{2(4)}$ or $x = -\dfrac{1}{2}$
   d. Given a curve $y = ax^2 + bx + c$, state the coordinates of the vertex or the turning point.
   Coordinates of vertex $= \left(\dfrac{-b}{2a}, f\left(\dfrac{-b}{2a} \right) \right)$
   e. State the coordinates of the vertex of the curve
   $y = 2x^2 - 3x - 27$.
   Coordinates of vertex $= \left(\dfrac{-b}{2a}, f\left(\dfrac{-b}{2a} \right) \right)$
   $$= \left(\dfrac{-(-3)}{2(2)}, f\left(\dfrac{3}{4} \right) \right) = \left(\dfrac{3}{4}, 2\left(\dfrac{3}{4} \right)^2 - 3\left(\dfrac{3}{4} \right) - 27 \right)$$
   $$= \left(\dfrac{3}{4}, 2\left(\dfrac{3}{4} \right)^2 - 3\left(\dfrac{3}{4} \right) - 27 \right) = \left(\dfrac{3}{4}, -\dfrac{225}{8} \right)$$
   f. Given a curve $y = ax^2 + bx + c$, the y-intercept is c.
   g. What is the y-intercept for the curve $y = 9x^2 - 30x + 25$?
   The y-intercept for the curve $y = 9x^2 - 30x + 25$ is 25.

h. Given that the coordinates of the turning point of a quadratic graph are (a, b) then the quadratic equation is given by: $(x - a)^2 + b = 0$.

i. Given the coordinates of the turning point of a quadratic graph are $(-1, 5)$, state the quadratic equation.
Quadratic equation is : $(x + 1)^2 + 5 = 0$

9. SIMULTANEOUS EQUATIONS

a. Solve linear and quadratic equations:

$x^2 + y^2 = 20$ (1)
$y - x = 6$ (2)
Substitute $y = 6 + x$ in (1)
$x^2 + (6 + x)^2 = 20$
$x^2 + 36 + 12x + x^2 = 20$
$2x^2 + 12x + 16 = 0$
$\therefore x^2 + 6x + 8 = 0$
$\therefore (x + 2)(x + 4) = 0$
$\therefore x = -2, x = -4$
Substitute x in (2)
When $x = -2, y = 6 + (-2) = 4$
When $x = -4, y = 6 + (-4) = 2$
Solutions are:
$x = -2, y = 4$
$x = -4, y = 2$

b. Solve simultaneous equations:
$4x + 5y = 14$ (1)×3
$8x - 3y = 2$ (2)×5
Adding (1)×3 + (2)×5
$12x + 15y = 42$
$\underline{40x - 15y = 10}$
$52x = 52$
$\therefore x = 1$
Substituting $x = 1$ in (1)
$4(1) + 5y = 14$
$5y = 10$
$\therefore y = 2$

Solution is:

$x = 1, y = 2$

10. LINEAR INEQUALITIES

Solve and represent solutions on the number line.

a. $5 + 3x \geq 11$

$3x \geq 11 - 5$

$3x \geq 6$

$\therefore x \geq 2$

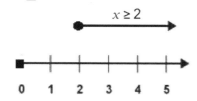

b. $4 \leq 5x - 6 < 14$

$4 + 6 \leq 5x < 14 + 6$

$10 \leq 5x < 20$

$\therefore 2 \leq x < 4$

c. $5 > 9 - 4x > 1$

$5 - 9 > -4x > 1 - 9$

$-4 > -4x > -8$

$-1 > -x > -2$

Removing negative signs and changing inequalities

$\therefore 1 < x < 2$

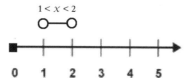

11. QUADRATIC INEQUALITIES

a. State the steps to solving a quadratic inequality.
   - i.   Solve the quadratic equation.
   - ii.   Sketch the graph.
   - iii. Use the sketch to find the solution.
   - iv.   For $y = f(x) > 0$, examine the graph above the $x -$ axis.

        For $y = f(x) < 0$, examine the graph below the $x -$ axis.

b. Solve the quadratic inequality $3x^2 + 2x - 1 > 0$
   Solving $3x^2 + 2x - 1 = 0$ we have,
   $(3x - 1)(x + 1) = 0$
   $\therefore x = \dfrac{1}{3}, x = -1$

   Sketch the graph using $\left(\dfrac{1}{3}, 0\right), (-1, 0)$ and $y -$intercept $(0, -1)$

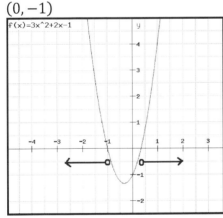

$\therefore 3x^2 + 2x - 1 > 0$, solution set is $x > \dfrac{1}{3}, x < -1$

c. Solve the quadratic inequality $x^2 - 5x + 6 < 0$
   Solving $x^2 - 5x + 6 = 0$ we have,
   $(x - 3)(x - 2) = 0$
   $\therefore x = 3, x = 2$
   Sketch the graph using $(2, 0), (3, 0)$ and $y -$intercept $(0, 6)$

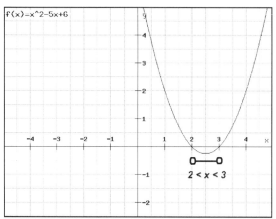

$\therefore x^2 - 5x + 6 < 0$, solution set is $2 < x < 3$.

d. Solve the quadratic inequality $8 - 2x \geq x^2$

Rearranging and solving $x^2 + 2x - 8 \leq 0$ we have,

$(x + 4)(x - 2) = 0$

$\therefore x = -4, x = 2$

Sketch the graph using $(-4, 0), (2, 0)$ and $y-$intercept $(0, -8)$

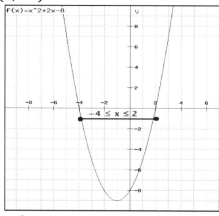

$\therefore x^2 + 2x - 8 \leq 0$, solution set is $-4 \leq x \leq 2$.

12. ALGEBRAIC FRACTIONS

a. Simplify $\dfrac{x^2-4x+4}{x^2-2x} \div \dfrac{x^2-4}{x-2}$

$$= \dfrac{x^2 - 4x + 4}{x^2 - 2x} \times \dfrac{x - 2}{x^2 - 4}$$

Factorising each expression we have,

$$= \dfrac{(x - 2)(x - 2)}{x(x - 2)} \times \dfrac{(x - 2)}{(x + 2)(x - 2)}$$

$$= \dfrac{(x - 2)}{x(x + 2)}$$

b. Solve for x: $\dfrac{2}{3x-1} + \dfrac{1}{x+8} = \dfrac{1}{2}$

$$\dfrac{4(x + 8) + 2(3x - 1)}{2(3x - 1)(x + 8)} = (3x - 1)(x + 8)$$

$$4x + 32 + 6x - 2 = 3x^2 + 23x - 8$$

$$3x^2 + 13x - 38 = 0$$

$$(3x + 19)(x - 2) = 0$$

$$\therefore x = -\dfrac{19}{3}, x = 2$$

13. SURDS

a. Define a surd.

A surd is a square root of a prime number.

b. Simplify the following: $2\sqrt{125} - 3\sqrt{20}$

$$= 2\sqrt{(5 \times 5) \times 5} - 3\sqrt{(2 \times 2) \times 5}$$

$$= 10\sqrt{5} - 6\sqrt{5}$$

$$= 4\sqrt{5}$$

c. What are the 3 rules of surds?

$$\sqrt{ab} = \sqrt{a} \times \sqrt{b}$$

$$\sqrt{a} \times \sqrt{a} = \sqrt{a \times a} = a$$

$$\sqrt{\dfrac{a}{b}} = \dfrac{\sqrt{a}}{\sqrt{b}}$$

d. Rationalise $\dfrac{15}{\sqrt{5}}$

$$= \frac{15}{\sqrt{5}} \times \frac{\sqrt{5}}{\sqrt{5}}$$

$$= \frac{15\sqrt{5}}{5}$$

$$= 3\sqrt{5}$$

e. Simplify: $(3 + \sqrt{2})(5 - 2\sqrt{2})$

$$(3 + \sqrt{2})(5 - 2\sqrt{2})$$
$$= 15 - 6\sqrt{2} + 5\sqrt{2} - 4$$
$$= 11 - \sqrt{2}$$

14. FACTOR THEOREM

a. Define the order of a polynomial.

The order of a polynomial is the highest power of x in the polynomial.

b. Divide by $(x^3 + 2x^2 - x - 2)$ by $(x - 1)$

$$
\begin{array}{r}
x^2 + 3x + 2 \\
\hline
x - 1\,\overline{)x^3 + 2x^2 - x - 2} \\
\mp x^3 \pm x^2 \\
\hline
+3x^2 - x \\
\mp 3x^2 \pm 3x \\
\hline
+2x + 2 \\
\mp 2x \pm 2 \\
\hline
\times
\end{array}
$$

$\therefore (x^3 + 2x^2 - x - 2) \div (x - 1) = x^2 + 3x + 2$

c. State the Factor Theorem.

If $f(x)$ is a polynomial and $f(a) = 0$, then $(x - a)$ is a factor of $f(x)$.

d. Factorise the following function $2x^3 + 7x^2 + 7x + 2$ as a product of 3 linear factors.

Check all factors of 2×2 ie. $\pm 1, \pm 2$

$f(-1) = -2 + 7 - 7 + 2 = 0$

$\therefore (x + 1)$ is a factor

$f(-2) = -16 + 28 - 14 + 2 = 0$

$\therefore (x + 2)$ is a factor

$(2x^3 + 7x^2 + 7x + 2) \div (x^2 + 3x + 2) = (2x + 1)$

Hence $2x^3 + 7x^2 + 7x + 2 = (x + 1)(x + 2)(2x + 1)$

e. Given that $f(x) = x^3 + 3x^2 - x - 3,$

     i.   Show that $(x + 1)$ is a factor of $f(x)$

            $f(-1) = -1 + 3 + 1 - 3 = 0$

            $\therefore (x + 1)$ is a factor of $f(x)$

     ii.   Factorise . $f(x)$

$$\begin{array}{r} x^2 + 2x - 3 \\ \hline x + 1\,|\,\overline{x^3 + 3x^2 - x - 3} \\ \underline{\mp x^3 \mp x^2} \\ +2x^2 - x \\ \underline{\mp 2x^2 \mp 2x} \\ -3x - 3 \\ \underline{\pm 3x + 3} \\ \times \end{array}$$

         $x^2 + 2x - 3 = (x + 3)(x - 1)$

         $\therefore x^3 + 3x^2 - x - 3 = (x + 1)(x - 1)(x + 3)$

     iii.   Solve $f(x) = 0$

         $(x + 1)(x - 1)(x + 3) = 0$

         $\therefore x = 1, -1, -3$

15. REMAINDER THEOREM

a. State the remainder theorem.

If a polynomial $f(x)$ is divided by $(ax - b)$ then the remainder is $f\left(\frac{b}{a}\right)$.

b. Find the remainder $x^3 - 3x^2 + 5x + 10$ is divided by $(x - 4)$.

$$
\begin{array}{r}
x^2 + x + 9 \\
\hline
x - 4 \,|\, x^3 - 3x^2 + 5x + 10 \\
\mp x^3 \pm 4x^2 \\
\hline
+ x^2 + 5x \\
\mp x^2 \pm 4x \\
\hline
+9x + 10 \\
\mp 9x \pm 36 \\
\hline
46
\end{array}
$$

Remainder= 46

$f(4) = (4)^3 - 3(4)^2 + 5(4) + 10 = 46$

c. When $x^3 + 4x^2 + ax + 6$ is divided by $(x + 5)$, the remainder is -4. What is a?

$f(-5) = -4$

$\therefore (-5)^3 + 4(-5)^2 + a(-5) + 6 = -4$

$-125 + 100 - 5a + 6 = -4$

$\therefore 5a = -15$

$\therefore a = -3$

Q&A IN BINOMIAL EXPANSION

1. **Define the binomial coefficient nC_r.**
2. **What is nC_0 and nC_n?**
3. Find $12C_5$.
4. **Expand $(1+x)^n$**
5. Expand the following: $(1+2x)^4$
6. **Expand $(a+b)^n$**
7. Expand the following: $(3x-4y)^3$
8. **Define the coefficient of any term in a binomial expansion.**
9. Find the coefficient of x^5 in the expansion $(1-3x)^9$.
10. Find the coefficient of a^3b^5 in the expansion $(a+2b)^8$.
11. **Describe the features of a binomial distribution.**
12. **Define the binomial distribution $P(X=r)$.**
    Describe the terms p, q and n.
13. **Describe the notation $X{\sim}B(n,p)$.**
14. For $X{\sim}B(6,0.2)$, find
    a. $P(X=4)$
    b. $P(X \leq 1)$
15. In a game, 5 fair dice are thrown. Calculate the
    probability that
    a. No six is thrown.
    b. At least 2 sixes are thrown.

1. Define the binomial coefficient nC_r.

   $nC_r = \dfrac{n!}{r!(n-r)!}$ where $n! = n\times(n-1)\times...\times3\times2\times1$

   nC_r also written as $\binom{n}{r}$

2. $nC_0 = 1$

   $nC_n = 1$

3. Find $12C_5$.

   $12C_5 = \dfrac{12!}{5!\,7!} = 792$

4. Expand $(1+x)^n$

   $(1+x)^n = 1 + \binom{n}{1}x + \binom{n}{2}x^2 + .. + x^n$

   $(1+x)^n = 1 + nx + \dfrac{n(n-1)}{2!}x^2 + \dfrac{n(n-1)(n-2)}{3!}x^3$

   $... + x^n$

5. Expand the following: $(1+2x)^4$

   $(1+2x)^4$

   $= 1 + \binom{4}{1}(2x) + \binom{4}{2}(2x)^2 + \binom{4}{3}(2x)^3 + (2x)^4$

   $= 1 + 8x + 24x^2 + 32x^3 + 16x^4$

6. Expand $(a+b)^n$

   $(a+b)^n = \binom{n}{0}a^n + \binom{n}{1}a^{n-1}b + \binom{n}{2}a^{n-2}b^2 + .. + \binom{n}{n}b^n$

   $(a+b)^n = a^n + na^{n-1}b + \dfrac{n(n-1)}{2!}a^{n-2}b^2$

   $+ \dfrac{n(n-1)(n-2)}{3!}a^{n-3}b^3 ... + b^n$

7. Expand the following: $(3x-4y)^3$

   $(3x-4y)^3$

   $= (3x)^3 + \binom{3}{1}(3x)^2(-4y) + \binom{3}{2}(3x)(-4y)^2 + (-4y)^3$

   $= 27x^3 - 108x^2y + 144xy^2 - 64y^3$

8. Define the coefficient of any term in a binomial
    expansion.
    Coefficient of rth term of a binomial expansion $(a + b)^n$
    is $nC_r a^{n-r} b^r$.
    Coefficient of rth term of a binomial expansion $(1 + b)^n$
    is $nC_r b^r$.

9. Find the coefficient of x^5 in the expansion $(1 - 3x)^9$.
    Term containing $x^5 = 9C_5(-3x)^5 = -30618x^5$
    Coefficient of $x^5 = -30618$

10. Find the coefficient of $a^3 b^5$ in the expansion $(a + 2b)^8$.
    Term containing $a^3 b^5 = 8C_5 a^3 (2b)^5 = 1792 a^3 b^5$
    Coefficient of $a^3 b^5 = 1792$

11. A binomial distribution is characterized by the
    following features:
    a. There must be a fixed number of trials denoted
        by n.
    b. Each trial can have only two possible outcomes -
        success or failure.
    c. The outcomes of each trial must be independent
        of each other.
    d. The probability of a success must remain the
        same for each trial.

12. Define the binomial distribution $P(X = r)$.
    $P(X = r) = nC_r p^r q^{n-r}$ where r=0, 1, 2...n
    Here,
    The probability of a successful outcome is p.
    The probability of the outcome of a failure is q.
    There are n trials and the number is successes is
    denoted by X.

13. Describe the notation $X \sim B(n, p)$.
    X defines a binomial distribution for n trials where p is
    the probability of success in each trial.

14. With $X \sim B(6, 0.2)$, $n = 6$, $p = 0.2$, $q = 0.8$
   a. $P(X = 4) = 6C_4(0.2)^4(0.8)^2$
       $= 0.01536$
   b. $P(X \leq 1) = P(X = 0) + P(X = 1)$
       $= 6C_0(0.2)^0(0.8)^6 + 6C_1(0.2)^1(0.8)^5$
       $= 0.262144 + 0.393216$
       $= 0.65536$

15. $n = 5, p = \frac{1}{6}, q = \frac{5}{6}$
   a. No six is thrown.
       $$P(X = 0) = 5C_0\left(\frac{1}{6}\right)^0\left(\frac{5}{6}\right)^5$$
       $= 0.401877572$

   b. At least 2 sixes are thrown.
       $P(X \geq 2) = 1 - [P(X = 0) + P(X = 1)]$
       $$= 1 - \left[0.401877572 + 5C_1\left(\frac{1}{6}\right)^1\left(\frac{5}{6}\right)^4\right]$$
       $= 1 - [0.401877572 + 0.401877572]$
       $= 0.196244856$

Q&A IN COORDINATE GEOMETRY

COORDINATE GEOMETRY – LINES

1. **What are the coordinates of the midpoint of a line joining two points (x_1, y_1) and (x_2, y_2)?**
2. A is the point $(3, 7)$ and B is the point $(-1, 5)$. Find the coordinates of the midpoint of the line AB.
3. **What is the length of a line joining two points (x_1, y_1) and (x_2, y_2)?**
4. A is the point $(-2, 3)$ and B is the point $(3, -9)$. Find the length of the line AB.
5. **What is the gradient of a line joining two points (x_1, y_1) and (x_2, y_2)?**
6. A is the point $(4, 4)$ and B is the point $(0, 2)$. Find the gradient of the line AB
7. **State the equation of a line with gradient m and y −intercept.**
8. **What is the gradient of a line parallel to the line $y = mx + c$?**
9. **What is the gradient of a line perpendicular to the line $y = mx + c$?**
10. **What is the equation of a line with gradient m and passing through a point (x_1, y_1)?**
11. Find, in the form of $y = mx + c$, the equation of the straight line with gradient $\frac{4}{5}$ and passing through the point $(-2, -5)$..
12. **What is the equation of a line passing through two points (x_1, y_1) and (x_2, y_2)?**
13. Find, in the form of $ax + by + c = 0$, the equation of the straight line passing through two points $(2, 1)$ and $(7, -3)$.

14. **If the gradient of line 1 is m_1 and the gradient of line 2 is m_2, state the relation between their gradients if the two lines are parallel to each other.**

15. Find the gradient of the straight line that is parallel to the line $2x - 5y + 1 = 0$.

16. **If the gradient of line 1 is m_1 and the gradient of line 2 is m_2, state the relation between their gradients if the two lines are perpendicular to each other.**

17. Find the gradient of the straight line that is perpendicular to the line $3x + 4y = 1$.

COORDINATE GEOMETRY – CIRCLES

1. **State the equation of a circle with centre (a, b) and radius r.**

2. Find the coordinates of the centre and the radius of the circle $(x - 3)^2 + (y + 1)^2 = 9$

3. **State the equation of a circle in general form.**

4. Find the coordinates of the centre and the radius of the circle given the equation of the circle as:
$$x^2 + y^2 - 2x - 10y - 23 = 0$$

5. **State the equation of a circle with centre at the origin and radius r.**

6. Find the equation of the circle with centre $(0, 0)$ and radius 4.

7. **What is product of the slope of the tangent and the slope of the normal at a particular point on a curve?**

8. **How are the coordinates of the point of intersection of a tangent and a curve found?**

9. Find the coordinates of the points where the line $y = x - 4$ intersects the circle $x^2 + y^2 = 10$.

COORDINATE GEOMETRY – LINES

1. What are the coordinates of the midpoint of a line joining two points (x_1, y_1) and (x_2, y_2)?

    Coordinates of Midpoint= $\left(\frac{x_1+x_2}{2}, \frac{y_1+y_2}{2}\right)$

2. A is the point $(3, 7)$ and B is the point $(-1, 5)$. Find the coordinates of the midpoint of the line AB.

    Coordinates of midpoint of AB = $\left(\frac{3-1}{2}, \frac{7+5}{2}\right) = (1, 6)$

3. What is the length of a line joining two points (x_1, y_1) and (x_2, y_2)?

    $$d = \sqrt{(x_1 - x_2)^2 + (y_1 - y_2)^2}$$

4. A is the point $(-2, 3)$ and B is the point $(3, -9)$. Find the length of the line AB.

    $$AB = \sqrt{(-2 - 3)^2 + (3 + 9)^2} = \sqrt{25 + 144} = 13$$

5. What is the gradient of a line joining two points (x_1, y_1) and (x_2, y_2)?

    Gradient $= \frac{y_2-y_1}{x_2-x_1}$

6. A is the point $(4, 4)$ and B is the point $(0, 2)$. Find the gradient of the line AB.

    Gradient of AB $= \frac{y_2-y_1}{x_2-x_1} = \frac{4-2}{4-0} = \frac{1}{2}$

7. State the equation of a line with gradient m and y−intercept.

$$y = mx + c$$

8. What is the gradient of a line parallel to the line $y = mx + c$?

Gradient $= m$

9. What is the gradient of a line perpendicular to the line $y = mx + c$?

Gradient $= -\dfrac{1}{m}$

10. What is the equation of a line with gradient m and passing through a point (x_1, y_1)?

$$y - y_1 = m(x - x_1)$$

11. Find, in the form of $y = mx + c$, the equation of the straight line with gradient $\dfrac{4}{5}$ and passing through the point $(-2, -5)$.
$$y - y_1 = m(x - x_1)$$
$$y + 5 = \frac{4}{5}(x + 2)$$
$$y = \frac{4}{5}x + \frac{8}{5} - 5$$
$$\therefore y = \frac{4}{5}x - \frac{17}{5}$$

12. What is the equation of a line passing through two points (x_1, y_1) and (x_2, y_2)?

$$\frac{y - y_1}{y_2 - y_1} = \frac{x - x_1}{x_2 - x_1}$$

13. Find, in the form of $ax + by + c = 0$, the equation of the straight line passing through two points $(2, 1)$ and $(7, -3)$.

$$\frac{y - y_1}{y_2 - y_1} = \frac{x - x_1}{x_2 - x_1}$$

$$\frac{y - 1}{-3 - 1} = \frac{x - 2}{7 - 2}$$

$$\frac{y - 1}{-4} = \frac{x - 2}{5}$$

$$5(y - 1) = -4(x - 2)$$
$$5y - 5 = -4x + 8$$
$$\therefore 4x + 5y - 13 = 0$$

14. If the gradient of line 1 is m_1 and the gradient of line 2 is m_2, state the relation between their gradients if the two lines are parallel to each other.

$$m_1 = m_2$$

15. Find the gradient of the straight line that is parallel to the line $2x - 5y + 1 = 0$.
$$2x - 5y + 1 = 0$$
$$5y = 2x + 1$$
$$y = \frac{2}{5}x + \frac{1}{5}$$
$$\therefore \text{Gradient} = \frac{2}{5}$$

16. If the gradient of line 1 is m_1 and the gradient of line 2 is m_2, state the relation between their gradients if the two lines are perpendicular to each other.

$$m_1 \times m_2 = -1$$

17. Find the gradient of the straight line that is perpendicular to the line $3x + 4y = 1$.

$3x + 4y = 1$
$4y = -3x + 1$
$y = -\dfrac{3}{4}x + \dfrac{1}{4}$
∴ Gradient $= -\dfrac{3}{4}$

∴ Gradient of line perpendicular to it is $= \dfrac{4}{3}$

COORDINATE GEOMETRY – CIRCLES

1. State the equation of a circle with centre (a, b) and radius r.

$(x - a)^2 + (y - b)^2 = r^2$

2. Find the coordinates of the centre and the radius of the circle $(x - 3)^2 + (y + 1)^2 = 9$
Coordinates of centre are: $(3, -1)$
Radius $= \sqrt{9} = 3$

3. State the equation of a circle in general form.
$x^2 + y^2 + Ax + By + C = 0$

4. Find the coordinates of the centre and the radius of the circle given the equation of the circle as:
$x^2 + y^2 - 2x - 10y - 23 = 0$
Rearranging we have:
$(x^2 - 2x) + (y^2 - 10y) = 23$
Completing the square for x and y
$(x - 1)^2 - 1 + (y - 5)^2 - 25 = 23$
$(x - 1)^2 + (y - 5)^2 = 49$
Coordinates of centre are: $(1, 5)$
Radius $= \sqrt{49} = 7$

5. State the equation of a circle with centre at the origin and radius r.

   $x^2 + y^2 = r^2$

6. Find the equation of the circle with centre $(0, 0)$ and radius 4.

   $x^2 + y^2 = 16$

7. What is product of the slope of the tangent and the slope of the normal at a particular point on a curve?
   Slope of tangent $\times$ Slope of normal $= -1$

8. How are the coordinates of the points of intersection of a tangent and a curve found?

   The coordinates of the points of intersection of a tangent and a curve found by solving their two equations.

9. Find the coordinates of the points where the line $y = x - 4$ intersects the circle $x^2 + y^2 = 10$

   Substituting $y = x - 4$ in $x^2 + y^2 = 10$, we have
   $x^2 + (x - 4)^2 = 10$
   $x^2 + x^2 - 8x + 16 = 10$
   $2x^2 - 8x + 6 = 0$
   $x^2 - 4x + 3 = 0$
   $\therefore (x - 3)(x - 1) = 0$
   $\therefore x = 3, x = 1$
   Substituting x in $y = x - 4$
   When $x = 3, y = x - 4 = 3 - 4 = -1$
   When $x = 1, y = x - 4 = 1 - 4 = -3$
   $\therefore$ Coordinates of the points of intersection are: $(3, -1)$ and $(1, -3)$.

Q&A IN LINEAR PROGRAMMING

1. **State the inequality that describes the following when comparing x and a number n:**
   a. x is at least n
   b. x is at most n
   c. x is more than n
   d. x is less than n
   e. x is no more than n
   f. x is no less than n
   g. x is under n
   h. x is over n
2. **How are boundaries represented for $\leq$ and $\geq$?**
3. **How are boundaries represented for $<$ and $>$?**
4. **How do you specify a shading of a region?**
5. Shade the region $y \geq 3$
6. Shade the region $x < -2$
7. Shade the region $x + 2y \leq 6$
8. Shade the region $y - 5 \leq x$
9. **Define the feasible region.**
10. **What is an objective function?**
11. **Where will the maximum and minimum values of an objective function be found?**
12. **List 4 steps to solve Linear Programming problems.**
13. On the same axes, indicate the region for which the following inequalities hold. Shade the region not required.
    $x \geq 0$
    $y \geq 0$
    $2x + y \leq 40$
    $x + 3y \leq 30$
    Find the maximum value of $9x + 7y$.

14. For a school trip, 150 teachers and students need to travel by coach or minibus. Each coach can hold 30 passengers and each minibus can hold 15 passengers. There are only 9 drivers available.

Let the number of minibuses used be x and the number of coaches used be y.

Form two inequalities in x and y. from the information given.

Assuming the inequality $x \geq 0$, draw the inequalities on a graph.

Find

a. the combination of vehicles that uses all 9 drivers with the minimum number of spare seats.

b. The combination of vehicles which minimises the number of drivers and will carry all 150 passengers.

1. State the inequality that describes the following when comparing x and a number n:

    a. x is at least n $x \geq n$

    b. x is at most n $x \leq n$

    c. x is more than n $x > n$

    d. x is less than n $x < n$

    e. x is no more than n $x \leq n$

    f. x is no less than n $x \geq n$

    g. x is under n $x < n$

    h. x is over n $x > n$

2. Boundaries for $\leq$ and $\geq$ are represented by solid lines.
3. Boundaries for $<$ and $>$ are represented by dotted lines.
4. Shading of a region is done on the side not required.

5. Shade the region $y \geq 3$

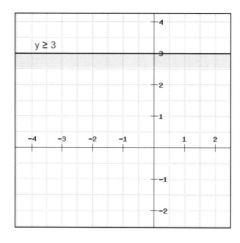

6. Shade the region $x < -2$

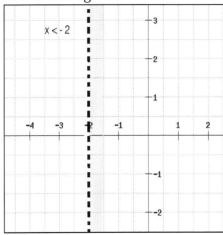

7. Shade the region $x + 2y \leq 6$

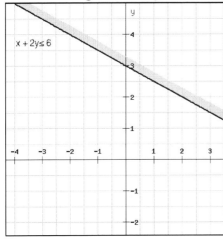

8. Shade the region $y - 5 \le x$

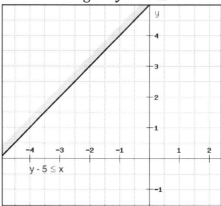

9. Define the feasible region.
   The region where a number of inequalities are
   simultaneously satisfied is called the feasible region.

10. What is an objective function?
    The objective function is an algebraic expression that is
    required to be maximised or minimised.

11. Where will the maximum and minimum values of an
    objective function be found?
    The maximum and minimum values of an objective
    function will lie at or near a vertex of the feasible
    region.

12. List 4 steps to solve Linear Programming problems.
    a. Choose the unknowns and write the system of
       inequalities.
    b. Represent the inequalities graphically and mark out
       the feasible region.
    c. Calculate the coordinates of the vertices of the
       feasible region.
    d. Find the value of the objective function at each of the
       vertices to determine its maximum or minimum
       value.

13. On the same axes, indicate the region for which the following inequalities hold. Shade the region not required.
    $x \geq 0$
    $y \geq 0$
    $2x + y \leq 40$
    $x + 3y \leq 30$
    Find the maximum value of $9x + 7y$.

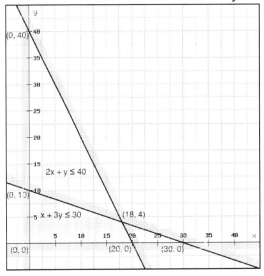

Vertices of feasible region are:
$(0, 0) \ (20, 0) \ (18, 4) \ (0, 10)$
$9x + 7y$ evaluated for each of the vertices is:
$= 0$ for $(0, 0)$
$= 180$ for $(20, 0)$
$= 190$ for $(18, 4)$
$= 70$ for $(0, 10)$
∴ the maximum value of $9x + 7y$ is 190

14. For a school trip, 150 teachers and students need to travel by coach or minibus. Each coach can hold 30 passengers and each minibus can hold 15 passengers. There are only 9 drivers available.
    Let the number of minibuses used be x and the number of coaches used be y.

Form two inequalities in x and y. from the information given.

Assuming the inequality $x \geq 0$, draw the inequalities on a graph.

Find

a. the combination of vehicles that uses all 9 drivers with the minimum number of spare seats.

b. The combination of vehicles which minimises the number of drivers and will carry all 150 passengers.

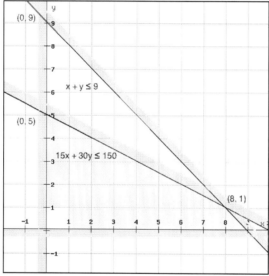

Number of minibuses $= x$

Number of coaches $= y$.

$15x + 30y \leq 150$

$x + y \leq 9$

a. The combination of vehicles that uses all 9 drivers with the minimum number of spare seats is 8 minibuses and 1 coach.

b. The combination of vehicles which minimises the number of drivers and will carry all 150 passengers is 5 coaches.

Q&A IN TRIGONOMETRY

1. **Sketch the graph of** $y = \sin\theta$ **for** $0° \leq \theta \leq 360°$
2. **Sketch the graph of** $y = \cos\theta$ **for** $0° \leq \theta \leq 360°$
3. **Sketch the graph of** $y = \tan\theta$ **for** $0° \leq \theta \leq 360°$. **State the equations of the asymptotes.**
4. **Given a right - angled triangle, state the trigonometric ratios for sine, cosine and tangent.**
5. Find the length x in each of the following triangles.

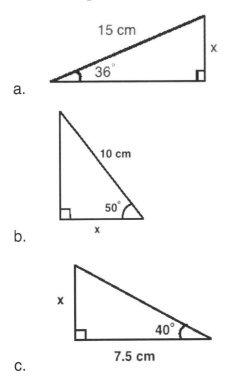

a.

b.

c.

6. **Given a right - angled triangle ABC right angled at C, state Pythagoras' Theorem.**

7. A ship sails 10 miles North and then 12 miles East. The ship returns to its starting point. Find the total distance the ship travels.
8. **State the sine rule to find an unknown side given two angles and one side.**
9. Find the length of the side x.

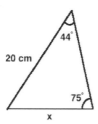

10. **State the sine rule to find an unknown angle given two sides and one angle.**
11. Find the size of the angle θ.

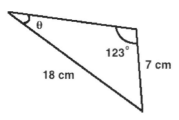

12. **State the cosine rule to find an unknown side given two sides and the included angle.**
13. Find the length of side x.

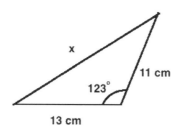

14. **State the cosine rule to find an unknown angle given three sides.**

15. Find the size of the angle θ.

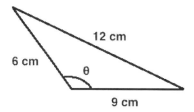

16. **State the formula to calculate the area of a triangle given two sides and the included angle.**

17. Find the area of the following triangle.

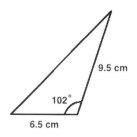

18. A ship P is 4 km away from a lighthouse on a bearing of 330°and a second ship Q is 5 km from the lighthouse on a bearing of 055°. Find the distance PQ between the ships.

19. **What are the 2 important identities linking sin θ, cos θ and tan θ?**

20. Factorise and solve the equation
$2 \sin^2 \theta + \sin \theta - 1 = 0$ for $0° \leq \theta \leq 360°$.

21. **Sketch the bow tie diagram and describe what can be deduced from it.**

22. Solve the following equations for $0° \leq \theta \leq 360°$.
   a. $\sin \theta = -0.5$
   b. $\cos \theta = 0.4$
   c. $\tan \theta = -7$

23. **What are the special trigonometric ratios for sin θ, cos θ and tan θ for 0° ≤ θ ≤ 360°?**
24. Solve the following equations for $0° \leq \theta \leq 360°$.
    a. $2 \cos \theta \tan \theta = 1$
    b. $1 + \sin \theta - 2 \cos^2 \theta = 0$
    c. $2 \sin \theta = \sqrt{3} \tan \theta$

1. The graph of $y = \sin\theta$ for $0° \leq \theta \leq 360°$

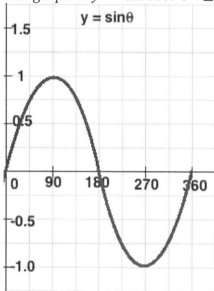

2. The graph of $y = \cos\theta$ for $0° \leq \theta \leq 360°$

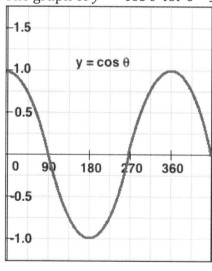

3. The graph of $y = \tan\theta$ for $0° \leq \theta \leq 360°$.

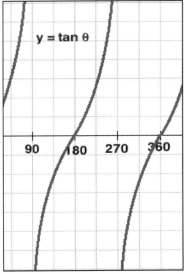

The vertical asymptotes are at $x = \pm90°, x = \pm270°$.

4. Given a right - angled triangle, the trigonometric ratios for sine, cosine and tangent are:

SOH-CAH-TOA

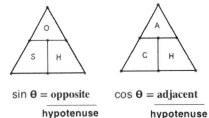

$\sin\theta = \dfrac{\text{opposite}}{\text{hypotenuse}}$ $\qquad$ $\cos\theta = \dfrac{\text{adjacent}}{\text{hypotenuse}}$ $\qquad$ $\tan\theta = \dfrac{\text{opposite}}{\text{adjacent}}$

5. Find the length x in each of the following triangles.
    a.

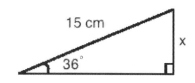

Using SOH, O = S×H
$x = \sin 36 \times 15 = 8.82$ cm

b.

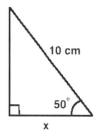

Using CAH, A = C×H
$x = \cos 50 \times 10 = 6.43$ cm

c.

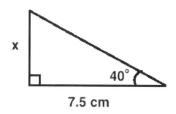

Using TOA, O = T×A
$x = \tan 40 \times 7.5 = 6.29$ cm

6. Given a right - angled triangle ABC right angled at C, state Pythagoras' Theorem.

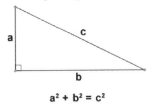

$$a^2 + b^2 = c^2$$

7. A ship sails 10 miles North and then 12 miles East. The ship returns to its starting point. Find the total distance the ship travels.

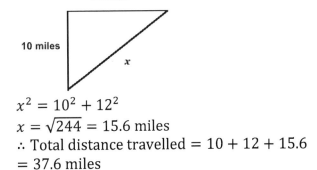

$x^2 = 10^2 + 12^2$
$x = \sqrt{244} = 15.6$ miles
$\therefore$ Total distance travelled $= 10 + 12 + 15.6$
$= 37.6$ miles

8. State the sine rule to find an unknown side given two angles and one side.

$$\frac{a}{\sin A} = \frac{b}{\sin B} = \frac{c}{\sin C}$$

9. Find the length of the side x.

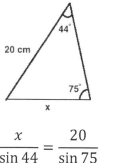

$$\frac{x}{\sin 44} = \frac{20}{\sin 75}$$

$$\therefore x = \frac{20 \sin 44}{\sin 75} = 14.4 \text{ cms (to 3 s f)}$$

10. State the sine rule to find an unknown angle given two
    sides and one angle.

$$\frac{\sin A}{a} = \frac{\sin B}{b} = \frac{\sin C}{c}$$

11. Find the size of the angle θ.

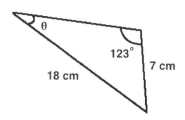

$$\frac{\sin \theta}{7} = \frac{\sin 123}{18}$$

$$\therefore \theta = sin^{-1}\left(\frac{7 \sin 123}{18}\right) = 19.04°$$

12. State the cosine rule to find an unknown side given two
    sides and the included angle.

$$a^2 = b^2 + c^2 - 2bc \cos A$$

13. Find the length of side x.

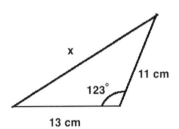

$$x^2 = 11^2 + 13^2 - 2(11)(13) \cos 123$$
$$x = \sqrt{121 + 169 - 286 \cos 123} = 21 \text{ cm (2 sf)}$$

14. State the cosine rule to find an unknown angle given three sides.

$$\cos A = \frac{b^2 + c^2 - a^2}{2bc}$$

15. Find the size of the angle θ.

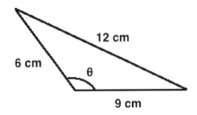

$$\cos \theta = \frac{6^2 + 9^2 - 12^2}{2(6)(9)} = -\frac{1}{4}$$
$$\cos^{-1}(0.25) = 75.5$$
$$\therefore \theta = 180 - 75.5 = 104.5°$$

16. State the formula to calculate the area of a triangle given two sides and the included angle.

Area of triangle$= \frac{1}{2} ab \sin C$

17. Find the area of the following triangle.

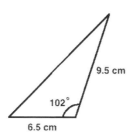

Area of triangle= $\frac{1}{2}(6.5)(9.5)sin\ 102$
= 30.2 $cm^2(to\ 3\ s\ f)$.

18. A ship P is 4 km away from a lighthouse on a bearing
    of 330°and a second ship Q is 5 km from the lighthouse
    on a bearing of 055°. Find the distance PQ between the
    ships.

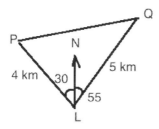

$PQ^2 = 4^2 + 5^2 - 2(4)(5)\cos 85$
$\therefore PQ = 6.12\ km\ (to\ 3\ sf)$

19. What are the 2 important identities linking sin θ, cos θ
    and tan θ?
    $sin^2\theta + cos^2\theta = 1$
    $tan\ \theta = \dfrac{sin\ \theta}{cos\ \theta}$

20. Factorise and solve the equation for
    2 sin² θ + sin θ − 1 = 0 for 0° ≤ θ ≤ 360°.
    Factorising we have:
    (2 sin θ − 1)(sin θ + 1) = 0

$$\therefore \sin\theta = \frac{1}{2}, \sin\theta = -1$$

$$\sin\theta = \frac{1}{2} \Rightarrow \theta = 30°, 150°$$

$$\sin\theta = -1 \Rightarrow \theta = 270°$$

21. Sketch the bow tie diagram and describe what can be deduced from it.

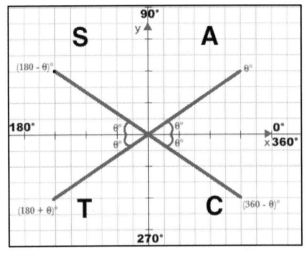

From the bow tie diagram we have the following facts:

a. In the first quadrant, sin, cos and tan are All positive.
    In the second quadrant, only Sin is positive.
    In the third quadrant, only Tan is positive.
    In the fourth quadrant, only Cos is positive.

b. Listing the angles for $0° \leq \theta \leq 360°$ we have:

	Positive values	Negative values
$\sin\theta°$	$\theta°, 180 - \theta°$	$360 - \theta°, 180 + \theta°$
$\cos\theta°$	$\theta°, 360 - \theta°,$	$180 + \theta°, 180 - \theta°$
$\tan\theta°$	$\theta°, 180 + \theta°$	$360 - \theta°, 180 - \theta°$

22. Solve the following equations for $0° \leq \theta \leq 360°$.
   a. $\sin \theta = -0.5$
       From the bow diagram there are 2 solutions for negative $\sin \theta$ namely: $360 - \theta°$ and $180 + \theta°$
       $$\theta = \sin^{-1}\left(\frac{1}{2}\right) = 30°$$
       The solution is therefore $\theta = 330°$ or $210°$

   b. $\cos \theta = 0.4$
       From the bow diagram there are 2 solutions for positive $\cos \theta$ namely: $\theta°$ and $360 - \theta°$
       $\theta = \cos^{-1}(0.4) = 66.4°$
       The solution is therefore $\theta = 66.4°$ or $293.6°$

   c. $\tan \theta = -7$
       From the bow diagram there are 2 solutions for negative $\tan \theta$ namely: $180 - \theta°$ and $360 - \theta°$
       $\theta = \tan^{-1}(7) = 81.9°$
       The solution is therefore $\theta = 98.1°$ or $278.1°$

23. What are the special trigonometric ratios for sin θ, cos θ and tan θ for $0° \leq \theta \leq 360°$?

θ	0°	30°	45°	60°	90°	180°	270°	360°
sin θ	0	$\frac{1}{2}$	$\frac{\sqrt{2}}{2}$	$\frac{\sqrt{3}}{2}$	1	0	-1	0
cos θ	1	$\frac{\sqrt{3}}{2}$	$\frac{\sqrt{2}}{2}$	$\frac{1}{2}$	0	-1	0	1
tan θ	0	$\frac{1}{\sqrt{3}}$	1	$\sqrt{3}$	undefined	0	undefined	0

24. Solve the following equations for $0° \leq \theta \leq 360°$.

a. $2 \cos \theta \tan \theta = 1$

$2 \cos \theta \dfrac{\sin \theta}{\cos \theta} = 1$

$2 \cos \theta \sin \theta = \cos \theta$

$2 \cos \theta \sin \theta - \cos \theta = 0$

$\cos \theta (2\sin \theta - 1) = 0$

$\sin \theta = \dfrac{1}{2}, \cos \theta = 0$

$\theta = \sin^{-1}\left(\dfrac{1}{2}\right)$

$\theta = 30°$

From the bow diagram there are 2 solutions for positive $\sin \theta$ namely: $\theta°$ and $180 - \theta°$

$\therefore \theta = 30°$ or $150°$

$\theta = \cos^{-1}(0)$

$\theta = 90°$

From the bow diagram there are 2 solutions for positive $\cos \theta$ namely: $\theta°$ and $360 - \theta°$

$\therefore \theta = 90°$ or $270°$

b. $1 + \sin \theta - 2 \cos^2 \theta = 0$

Replacing $\cos^2\theta$ by $1 - \sin^2 \theta$ we have,

$1 + \sin \theta - 2(1 - \sin^2 \theta) = 0$

$1 + \sin \theta - 2 + 2sin^2\theta = 0$

Solving $2sin^2\theta + \sin \theta - 1 = 0$

We have $(2\sin \theta - 1)(\sin \theta + 1) = 0$

$\sin \theta = \dfrac{1}{2} \Rightarrow \theta = 30°, 150°$

$\sin \theta = -1 \Rightarrow \theta = 270°$

c. $2 \sin \theta = \sqrt{3} \tan \theta$

$2 \sin \theta = \sqrt{3} \dfrac{\sin \theta}{\cos \theta}$

$2 \sin \theta - \sqrt{3} \dfrac{\sin \theta}{\cos \theta} = 0$

$$\sin \theta \left(2 - \frac{\sqrt{3}}{\cos \theta} \right) = 0$$

$\therefore \sin \theta = 0 \implies \theta = 0°, 180°$

$\therefore \cos \theta = \frac{\sqrt{3}}{2} \implies \theta = 30°, 330°$

Q&A IN 3D TRIG PROBLEMS

1. **Define a plane in 3D space.**
2. **How do you find the angle between a line and a plane?**
3. **How do you find the angle between two planes- also known as the angle of greatest slope?**
4. ABCDFE is a wedge with AB 50 cm, CE 10 cm and angle EBC is 30°.

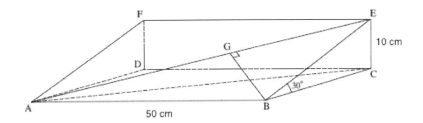

Find
a. BE
b. Angle EAC
c. Area of triangle ABE
d. BG

1. Define a plane in 3D space.
    A plane in 3D space is a flat surface.

2. How do you find the angle between a line and a plane?

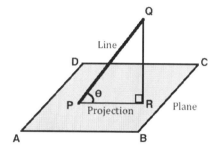

The angle θ between the line PQ and the plane ABCD is angle between the line PQ and its projection PR on the plane.

3. How do you find the angle between two planes- also known as the angle of greatest slope?

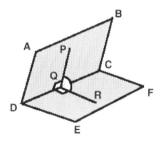

Two planes ABCD and CDEF intersect in line CD. Point P lies on the plane of ABCD and PQ ⊥ CD. Point R lies on the plane of CDEF and QR ⊥ CD. Angle PQR is the angle between the two planes. If plane CDEF is a horizontal plane, then PQ is a line of greatest slope in plane ABCD.

5. ABCDFE is a wedge with AB 50 cm, CE 10 cm and angle EBC is 30°.

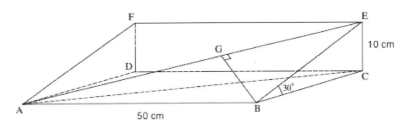

a. Consider Δ EBC,

$$\sin 30 = \frac{10}{BE}$$

$$BE = \frac{10}{\sin 30} = 20 \text{ cm}$$

b. Consider Δ AEB,
$$AE^2 = BE^2 + AB^2$$
$$AE = \sqrt{20^2 + 50^2} = 53.8516 \text{ cm}$$
Consider Δ EAC,
$$\sin EAC = \frac{10}{AE} = \frac{10}{53.8516}$$
$$\angle EAC = \sin^{-1}(0.185695) = 10.7°$$

c. Area of triangle ABE$= \frac{1}{2} \times AB \times BE = \frac{1}{2} \times 50 \times 20$
$= 500 \ cm^2$

d. Area of triangle ABE$= \frac{1}{2} \times AE \times BG = 500$
$$\therefore BG = \frac{500 \times 2}{AE} = 18.6 \text{ cm}$$

Q&A IN CALCULUS

DIFFERENTIATION
1. **Define the first order derivative of a curve $y = f(x)$.**
2. **Given that $y = f(x) = x^n$, what is the first order derivative $\frac{dy}{dx}$ or $f'(x)$?**
3. **Given that $y = f(x) = ax^n$, what is the first order derivative $\frac{dy}{dx}$ or $f'(x)$?**
4. Find the $\frac{dy}{dx}$ for the curve $y = 3x(x^2 + \frac{4}{x} - 1)$.
5. **Define the second order derivative of a curve $y = f(x)$..**
6. Find the $\frac{d^2y}{dx^2}$ for the curve $y = 2x^3 - 7x^2 + x - 11$
7. **Define a stationary point.**
8. **Name, sketch and describe the 3 stationary points.**
9. **Describe the 3 steps to finding the coordinates of the stationary points of a curve and determining their nature.**
10. Find the position and nature of any stationary points of the curve
$y = 2x^3 - 15x^2 + 24x + 8$.
Sketch the curve.
11. Given the curve $f(x) = 3x^2 - x^3$ with a point P $(1, 2)$ on the curve. Find
   a. the gradient function $\frac{dy}{dx}$
   b. the gradient of the curve at P.
   c. the equation of the tangent at P.
   d. the equation of the normal at P.

INTEGRATION

1. **What is integration?**
2. **For $\frac{dy}{dx} = x^n$, define $y = \int x^n dx$.**
3. **For $\frac{dy}{dx} = ax^n$, define $y = \int ax^n dx$.**
4. Given the gradient function $\frac{dy}{dx} = 3x^5 - x^3 + 4x - 1$ find $y = f(x)$.
5. Find the indefinite integral $\int (x - 3)^2 dx$
6. **How can the constant of integration c be determined?**
7. For the gradient function $\frac{dy}{dx} = 2x - 5$ find the equation of the curve $y = f(x)$ that passes through the point $(1, 2)$.
8. **Define a definite integral.**
9. Evaluate the definite integral $\int_{-1}^{2} (x^3 - 2) \, dx$.
10. **How do you compute the area between a curve $y = f(x)$, the x – axis and the lines $x = a$ and $x = b$?**
11. Find the area between the curve $y = 12 - x - x^2$ and the x – axis between $x = 0$ and $x = 3$. Sketch and shade the computed area.
12. **How do you compute the area between a curve y_1 and a curve y_2?**
13.
    a. Sketch the graph of the two curves $y = x^2 - 16$ and $y = 4x - x^2$.
    b. Find the x coordinates of the points of intersection.
    c. Find the area enclosed by the two curves.

DIFFERENTIATION

1. Define the first order derivative of a curve $y = f(x)$.
    The first order derivative $f'(x)$ is the slope or gradient
    of a curve $y = f(x)$ at a point on the curve. $f'(x)$ is the
    slope of the tangent at any point on the curve.

2. Given that $y = f(x) = x^n$, what is the first order
    derivative $\frac{dy}{dx}$ or $f'(x)$?
    If $y = f(x) = x^n$
    $$\frac{dy}{dx} = f'(x) = nx^{n-1}$$

3. Given that $y = f(x) = ax^n$, what is the first order
    derivative $\frac{dy}{dx}$ or $f'(x)$?
    If $y = f(x) = ax^n$
    $$\frac{dy}{dx} = f'(x) = nax^{n-1}$$

4. Find the $\frac{dy}{dx}$ for the curve $y = 3x(x^2 + \frac{4}{x} - 1)$.
    $$y = 3x(x^2 + \frac{4}{x} - 1)$$
    $$y = 3x^3 + 12 - 3x$$
    $$\therefore \frac{dy}{dx} = 9x^2 - 3$$

5. Define the second order derivative of a curve
    $y = f(x)$.
    The second order derivative $f''(x) = \frac{d^2y}{dx^2}$ is the
    derivative of the derivative $f'(x)$ and denotes the
    concavity or convexity of the curve.

6. Find the $\frac{d^2y}{dx^2}$ for the curve $y = 2x^3 - 7x^2 + x - 11$

$y = 2x^3 - 7x^2 + x - 11$

$\frac{dy}{dx} = 6x^2 - 14x + 1$

$\therefore \frac{d^2y}{dx^2} = 12x - 14$

7. Define a stationary point.

When the gradient or slope of the curve is 0, the curve is at a stationary point.

8. Name, sketch and describe the 3 stationary points.

The stationary point is a maximum point if

$\frac{dy}{dx} = 0$ and $\frac{d^2y}{dx^2} < 0$

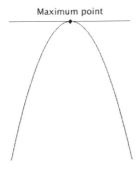

Maximum point

The stationary point is a minimum point if

$\frac{dy}{dx} = 0$ and $\frac{d^2y}{dx^2} > 0$

Minimum point

The stationary point is an inflexion point if
$\frac{dy}{dx} = 0$ and $\frac{d^2y}{dx^2} = 0$

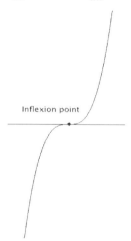

Inflexion point

9. Describe the 3 steps to finding the coordinates of the stationary points of a curve and determining their nature.

In order to find the coordinates of the stationary points of a graph:

a. Equate $\frac{dy}{dx}$ to 0 and solve the function.

b. For each x, find the corresponding y.

c. Compute $\frac{d^2y}{dx^2}$ for each x.

- If $\frac{d^2y}{dx^2} < 0$, the stationary point is a maximum point.

- If $\frac{d^2y}{dx^2} > 0$, the stationary point is a minimum point.

- If $\frac{d^2y}{dx^2} = 0$, the stationary point is an inflexion point which is confirmed if $\frac{d^3y}{dx^3} \neq 0$

10. Find the position and nature of any stationary points of the curve $y = 2x^3 - 15x^2 + 24x + 8$. Sketch the curve.

$y = 2x^3 - 15x^2 + 24x + 8$

$\frac{dy}{dx} = 6x^2 - 30x + 24 = 0$

$2x^2 - 10x + 8 = 0$

$(2x - 2)(x - 4) = 0$

$\therefore x = 1, 4$

For $x = 1, y = 19$

For $x = 4, y = -8$

$(1, 19)$ and $(4, -8)$ are stationary points.

$\frac{d^2y}{dx^2} = 12x - 30$

At $(1, 19), \frac{d^2y}{dx^2} = 12 - 30 = -18 < 0$

$\therefore (1, 19)$ is a maximum point.

At $(4, -8), \frac{d^2y}{dx^2} = 48 - 30 = 18 > 0$

$\therefore (4, -8)$ is a minimum point.

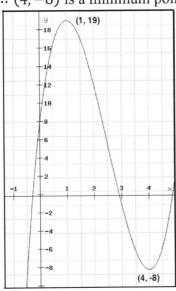

11. Given the curve $f(x) = 3x^2 - x^3$ with a point P $(1, 2)$ on the curve. Find
   a. the gradient function $\frac{dy}{dx}$
   b. the gradient of the curve at P.
   c. the equation of the tangent at P.
   d. the equation of the normal at P.

a. $y = 3x^2 - x^3$

$$\therefore \frac{dy}{dx} = 6x - 3x^2$$

b. At P, $x = 1$,

$$\therefore \frac{dy}{dx} = 6(1) - 3(1)^2 = 6 - 3 = 3$$

c. The equation of the tangent is given by the equation
   $y - y_1 = m(x - x_1)$
   Point P is $(1, 2)$ and m $= 3$
   $y - 2 = 3(x - 1)$
   $\therefore y = 3x - 1$ is the equation of the tangent to the curve at P.

d. The equation of the normal is given by the equation
   $y - y_1 = m_1(x - x_1)$ where $m_1 = -\frac{1}{m}$
   Point P is $(1, 2)$ and $m_1 = -\frac{1}{3}$
   $y - 2 = -\frac{1}{3}(x - 1)$
   $\therefore y = -\frac{1}{3}x + \frac{7}{3}$ is the equation of the normal to the curve at P.

INTEGRATION

1. What is integration?
   Integration is the reverse of differentiation.
2. For $\frac{dy}{dx} = x^n$, define $y = \int x^n dx$.

   If $\frac{dy}{dx} = x^n$

   then $y = \frac{x^{n+1}}{(n+1)} + c$

   where c is the constant of integration.

3. For $\frac{dy}{dx} = ax^n$, define $y = \int ax^n dx$.

   If $\frac{dy}{dx} = ax^n$

   then $y = \frac{ax^{n+1}}{(n+1)} + c$

   where c is the constant of integration.

4. Given the gradient function $\frac{dy}{dx} = 3x^5 - x^3 + 4x - 1$ find
   $y = f(x)$.

   $$y = \int (3x^5 - x^3 + 4x - 1)\, dx$$

   $$= \frac{3x^6}{6} - \frac{x^4}{4} + \frac{4x^2}{2} - x + c$$

   $$\therefore y = \frac{x^6}{2} - \frac{x^4}{4} + 2x^2 - x + c$$

5. Find the indefinite integral $\int (x - 3)^2 dx$

   $$y = \int (x - 3)^2 dx$$

   $$y = \int (x^2 - 6x + 9)dx$$

   $$y = \frac{x^3}{3} - \frac{6x^2}{2} + 9x + c$$

   $$\therefore y = \frac{x^3}{3} - 3x^2 + 9x + c$$

6. How can the constant of integration c be determined?
   The constant of integration c can be determined for any curve $y = f(x)$ if you are given any point (x, y) that the curve passes through.

7. For the gradient function $\frac{dy}{dx} = 2x - 5$ find the equation of the curve $y = f(x)$ that passes through the point $(1, 2)$.

   $\frac{dy}{dx} = 2x - 5$

   $\therefore y = \frac{2x^2}{2} - 5x + c$

   $y = x^2 - 5x + c$

   At point$(1, 2)$

   $2 = 1 - 5 + c$

   $\therefore c = 6$

   Hence the equation of the curve is

   $y = x^2 - 5x + 6$

8. Define a definite integral.
   The definite integral is an integral with its upper and lower limits defined. It is defined as

   $$\int_a^b f'(x)dx = [f(x)]_a^b$$

   $= f(b) - f(a)$

   where $f'(x)$ is the derived function of $f(x)$ over the interval (a, b).

9. Evaluate the definite integral $\int_{-1}^2 (x^3 - 2)\, dx$.

   $$\int_{-1}^2 (x^3 - 2)\, dx = \left[\frac{x^4}{4} - 2x\right]_{-1}^2$$

   $$= \left[\frac{2^4}{4} - 2(2)\right] - \left[\frac{(-1)^4}{4} - 2(-1)\right]$$

   $$= 0 - \frac{9}{4} = -\frac{9}{4}$$

10. How do you compute the area between a curve $y =$ $f(x)$, the x - axis and the lines $x = a$ and $x = b$?

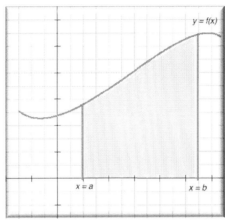

The area between a curve $y = f(x)$, the x - axis and the lines $x = a$ and $x = b$ is given by:

Area = $\int_a^b y \, dx$

11. Find the area between the curve $y = 12 - x - x^2$ and the x - axis between $x = 0$ and $x = 3$. Sketch and shade the computed area.

Area = $\int_0^3 12 - x - x^2 \, dx$

$= \left[12x - \frac{x^2}{2} - \frac{x^3}{3} \right]_0^3$

$= \left[12(3) - \frac{3^2}{2} - \frac{3^3}{3} \right] = 22.5 \text{ units}^2$

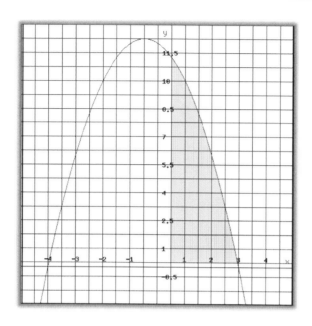

12. How do you compute the area between a curve y_1 and a curve y_2?

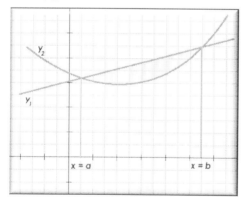

The area between a line $\boldsymbol{y_1}$ and a curve $\boldsymbol{y_2}$ is given by:

Area = $\int_a^b (y_1 - y_2)dx$

The points of intersection of the line and the curve are determined algebraically by solving for x by equating the expressions : $y_1 = y_2$

13.

    a. Sketch the graph of the two curves $y = x^2 - 16$ and $y = 4x - x^2$.

    b. Find the x coordinates of the points of intersection.

    c. Find the area enclosed by the two curves.

a.

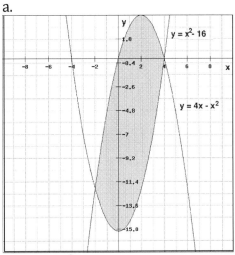

b. $y = x^2 - 16$
    $y = 4x - x^2$
    $\therefore x^2 - 16 = 4x - x^2$
    $2x^2 - 4x - 16 = 0$
    $x^2 - 2x - 8 = 0$
    $(x - 4)(x + 2) = 0$
    $\therefore x = -2, 4$

c. Area=$\int_{-2}^{4}(y_1 - y_2)dx$

$$= \int_{-2}^{4} (4x - x^2) - (x^2 - 16)dx$$

$$= \int_{-2}^{4} (4x - 2x^2 + 16)dx$$

$$= \left[\frac{4x^2}{2} - \frac{2x^3}{3} + 16x \right]_{-2}^{4} = \frac{160}{3} + \frac{56}{3} = 72 \text{ units}^2$$

Q&A IN KINEMATICS

1. Define the symbols s, u, v, a and t and state the SI units for each.
2. For a particle moving horizontally in a straight line with constant acceleration, which movement makes the displacement and velocity positive and which movement makes the displacement and velocity negative?
3. If a particle is slowing down describe its acceleration.
4. State the 5 formulae used in solving problems about particles moving in a straight line with constant acceleration.
5. A vehicle, initially moving at 45 ms^{-1} brakes and comes to rest with constant deceleration in 15 seconds.
   a. Find the deceleration.
   b. Find the distance travelled in this time.
6. What is the acceleration due to gravity?
7. Define time of flight in a projection.
8. Define speed of projection.
9. A ball is projected vertically upwards from a point P. The greatest height reached by the ball is 40m above P. Calculate
   a. The speed of projection.
   b. The time of flight before the ball returns to P.
10. In the case of motion with variable acceleration, state the relation between the acceleration a, the velocity v, the distance s and the time t.

11. A body moves in a straight line such that at time t its displacement, s, from the fixed point O is given by
$$s = 4t^3 - 3t + 5$$
   a. Find expressions for the velocity and acceleration at time t.
   b. Find the time and position when velocity is 0.

12. The velocity $v\ ms^{-1}$ of a particle at time t seconds is given by $v = t^3 - 4t^2 + 4t + 2$
   a. Find an expression for the acceleration $a\ ms^{-2}$ in terms of t.
   b. Find the distance travelled in 4 seconds.

1. Define the symbols s, u, v, a and t and state the SI units for each.

s	Distance/Displacement	metres	m
u	Initial velocity	metres per second	ms^{-1}
v	Final velocity	metres per second	ms^{-1}
a	Constant acceleration	$metres/second^2$	ms^{-2}
t	Time	seconds	s

2. For a particle moving horizontally in a straight line with constant acceleration, displacement and velocity are positive when the particle moves from left to right and negative when the particle moves from right to left.

3. If a particle is slowing down it has negative acceleration or deceleration

4. State the 5 formulae used in solving problems about particles moving in a straight line with constant acceleration.

$$v = u + at$$
$$s = \frac{(u + v)t}{2}$$
$$v^2 = u^2 + 2as$$
$$s = ut + \frac{1}{2}at^2$$
$$s = vt - \frac{1}{2}at^2$$

5. A vehicle, initially moving at 45 ms^{-1} brakes and comes to rest with constant deceleration in 15 seconds.
   a. $v = 0$, $u = 45$, $t = 15$
   Use $v = u + at$
   $0 = 45 + 15a$
   $a = -3\ ms^{-1}$
   $\therefore$ Deceleration $= 3\ ms^{-1}$
   b. Find the distance travelled in this time.
   Use $S = \dfrac{(u+v)t}{2}$

   $$S = \frac{(45+0)15}{2} = 337.5\ m$$

6. What is the acceleration due to gravity?
   For a particle moving vertically in a straight line with constant acceleration, we have the following:
   a. There is a constant downward acceleration due to gravity $g = 9.8\ ms^{-1}$.
   b. When solving problems about vertical motion, the positive direction can be chosen to be either upwards or downwards.
   c. For objects projected upwards, $g = -9.8\ ms^{-1}$. For falling objects, $g = +9.8\ ms^{-1}$.

7. Define time of flight in a projection.
   The total time that an object is in motion from the time it is projected upwards to the time it hits the ground is called the time of flight.

8. Define speed of projection.
   The initial speed is called the speed of projection.

9. A ball is projected vertically upwards from a point P.
    The greatest height reached by the ball is 40m above P.
    a. $v = 0, a = -9.8\ ms^{-1},\ s = 40m$
        Use $v^2 = u^2 + 2as$

        $0^2 = u^2 + 2(-9.8)(40)$
        $u^2 = 784$
        $u = \sqrt{784} = 28$
        ∴ Speed of projection $= 28\ ms^{-1}$
    b. Total time of flight = time of ascent + time of
        descent = 2× (time of ascent)
        $a = -9.8\ ms^{-1}, u = 28\ ms^{-1}, v = 0$
        Use $v = u + at$ to calculate time of ascent
        $9.8t = 28$
        $t = 2.8571$
        ∴ Time of flight $= 2t = 5.71\ s$

10. In the case of motion with variable acceleration, state
    the relation between the acceleration a, the velocity v,
    the displacement s and the time t.
    a. Given the displacement, s, as a function of t:
        $$v = \frac{ds}{dt} \text{ and } a = \frac{dv}{dt}$$
    b. Given the acceleration, a, as a function of t:
        $$v = \int a\, dt \text{ and } s = \int v\, dt$$

11. A body moves in a straight line such that at time t its
    displacement, s, from the fixed point O is given by
    $s = 4t^3 - 3t + 5$
    a. Velocity $v = \frac{ds}{dt} = 12t^2 - 3$

        Acceleration $a = \frac{dv}{dt} = 24t$

    b. Find the time and position when velocity is 0.
        $12t^2 - 3 = 0$
        $t^2 = \frac{1}{4}$

$$\therefore t = \frac{1}{2}\sec$$
$$s = 4t^3 - 3t + 5 = 4(0.5)^3 - 3(0.5) + 5$$
$$\therefore s = 4\,m$$

13. The velocity v ms^{-1} of a particle at time t seconds is given by $v = t^3 - 4t^2 + 4t + 2$
   a. Acceleration $a = \frac{dv}{dt} = 3t^2 - 8t + 4$.
   b. $s = \int v\,dt = \int(t^3 - 4t^2 + 4t + 2)\,dt$
   $$s = \frac{t^4}{4} - \frac{4t^3}{3} + \frac{4t^2}{2} + 2t + c$$
   $$s = \frac{t^4}{4} - \frac{4t^3}{3} + 2t^2 + 2t + c$$
   When $t = 0, s = 0$, hence $c = 0$
   $$\therefore s = \frac{t^4}{4} - \frac{4t^3}{3} + 2t^2 + 2t$$
   Distance travelled in 4 seconds
   $$= \frac{(4)^4}{4} - \frac{4(4)^3}{3} + 2(4)^2 + 2(4)$$
   $$= \frac{56}{3} = 18\frac{2}{3}m$$

RAPID REVISION QUIZ

ALGEBRA
1. State the three methods of factorisation.
2. Difference of 2 squares: $x^2 - y^2 =$
3. State the rules for change of subject of formula.
4. List three methods for solving quadratic equations.
5. Completing the square formula: $x^2 + bx =$
6. Quadratic formula: $x =$
7. Describe FOIL expansion for multiplying expressions.
8. Expansion: $(x + y)(x - y) =$
9. Expansion: $(x + y)^2 =$
10. Expansion: $(x - y)^2 =$
11. Given a curve $y = ax^2 + bx + c$, state the line of symmetry.
12. Given a curve $y = ax^2 + bx + c$, state the coordinates of the vertex or the turning point.
13. Given a curve $y = ax^2 + bx + c$, what is the y-intercept?
14. Given that the coordinates of the turning point of a quadratic graph are (a, b) the quadratic equation is given by:_____.
15. State the steps to solving a quadratic inequality.
16. Define a surd.
17. What are the 3 rules of surds?
18. Define the order of a polynomial.
19. State the factor theorem.
20. State the remainder theorem.

BINOMIAL EXPANSION
1. Define the binomial coefficient nC_r.
2. What is nC_0 and nC_n?
3. Expand $(1 + x)^n$
4. Expand $(a + b)^n$
5. Define the coefficient of any term in a binomial expansion.
6. Describe the features of a binomial distribution.
7. Define the binomial distribution $P(X = r)$.
8. Describe the notation $X \sim B(n, p)$.

COORDINATE GEOMETRY – LINES

1. What are the coordinates of the midpoint of a line joining two points (x_1, y_1) and (x_2, y_2)?
2. What is the length of a line joining two points (x_1, y_1) and (x_2, y_2)?
3. What is the gradient of a line joining two points (x_1, y_1) and (x_2, y_2)?
4. State the equation of a line with gradient m and y –intercept.
5. What is the gradient of a line parallel to the line $y = mx + c$?
6. What is the gradient of a line perpendicular to the line $y = mx + c$?
7. What is the equation of a line with gradient m and passing through a point (x_1, y_1)?
8. What is the equation of a line passing through two points (x_1, y_1) and (x_2, y_2)?
9. If the gradient of line 1 is m_1 and the gradient of line 2 is m_2, state the relation between their gradients if the two lines are parallel to each other.
10. If the gradient of line 1 is m_1 and the gradient of line 2 is m_2, state the relation between their gradients if the two lines are perpendicular to each other.

COORDINATE GEOMETRY – CIRCLES

1. State the equation of a circle with centre (a, b) and radius r.
2. State the equation of a circle in general form.
3. State the equation of a circle with centre at the origin and radius r.
4. What is product of the slope of the tangent and the slope of the normal at a particular point on a curve?
5. How are the coordinates of the point of intersection of a tangent and a curve found?

LINEAR PROGRAMMING

1. State the inequality that describes the following when comparing x and a number n:
   a. x is at least n
   b. x is at most n
   c. x is more than n
   d. x is less than n
   e. x is no more than n
   f. x is no less than n
   g. x is under n
   h. x is over n
2. How are boundaries represented for $\leq$ and $\geq$?
3. How are boundaries represented for $<$ and $>$?
4. How do you specify a shading of a region?
5. Define the feasible region.
6. What is an objective function?
7. Where will the maximum and minimum values of an objective function be found?
8. List 4 steps to solve Linear Programming problems.

TRIGONOMETRY

1. Sketch the graph of $y = \sin \theta$ for $0° \leq \theta \leq 360°$
2. Sketch the graph of $y = \cos \theta$ for $0° \leq \theta \leq 360°$
3. Sketch the graph of $y = \tan \theta$ for $0° \leq \theta \leq 360°$. State the equations of the asymptotes.
4. Given a right - angled triangle, state the trigonometric ratios for sine, cosine and tangent.
5. Given a right - angled triangle ABC right angled at C, state Pythagoras' Theorem.
6. State the sine rule to find an unknown side given two angles and one side.
7. State the sine rule to find an unknown angle given two sides and one angle.
8. State the cosine rule to find an unknown side given two sides and the included angle.
9. State the cosine rule to find an unknown angle given three sides.
10. State the formula to calculate the area of a triangle given two sides and the included angle.
11. What are the 2 important identities linking $\sin \theta$, $\cos \theta$ and $\tan \theta$?
12. Sketch the bow tie diagram and describe what can be deduced from it.
13. What are the special trigonometric ratios for $\sin \theta$, $\cos \theta$ and $\tan \theta$ for $0° \leq \theta \leq 360°$?

3D TRIGONOMETRY PROBLEMS

1. Define a plane in 3D space.
2. How do you find the angle between a line and a plane?
3. How do you find the angle between two planes- also known as the angle of greatest slope?

CALCULUS
DIFFERENTIATION

1. Define the first order derivative of a curve $y = f(x)$.
2. Given that $y = f(x) = x^n$, what is the first order derivative $\frac{dy}{dx}$ or $f'(x)$?
3. Given that $y = f(x) = ax^n$, what is the first order derivative $\frac{dy}{dx}$ or $f'(x)$?
4. Define the second order derivative of a curve $y = f(x)$.
5. Define a stationary point.
6. Name, sketch and describe the 3 stationary points.
7. Describe the 3 steps to finding the coordinates of the stationary points of a curve and determining their nature.

INTEGRATION

1. What is integration?
2. For $\frac{dy}{dx} = x^n$, define $y = \int x^n dx$.
3. For $\frac{dy}{dx} = ax^n$, define $y = \int ax^n dx$.
4. How can the constant of integration c be determined?
5. Define a definite integral.
6. How do you compute the area between a curve $y = f(x)$, the x – axis and the lines $x = a$ and $x = b$?
7. How do you compute the area between a curve y_1 and a curve y_2?

KINEMATICS

1. Define the symbols s, u, v, a and t and state the SI units for each.
2. For a particle moving horizontally in a straight line with constant acceleration, which movement makes the displacement and velocity positive and which movement makes the displacement and velocity negative?
3. If a particle is slowing down describe its acceleration.
4. State the 5 formulae used in solving problems about particles moving in a straight line with constant acceleration.
5. What is the acceleration due to gravity?
6. Define time of flight in a projection.
7. Define speed of projection.
8. In the case of motion with variable acceleration, state the relation between the acceleration a, the velocity v, the distance s and the time t.

ABOUT THE AUTHOR

Shobha Natarajan holds an MSc in Mathematics from Bangalore University and teaches Mathematics to students at A Level and GCSE in the Medway towns of Kent. The Maths Clinic was established in 2011 to publish revision guides in Mathematics in print and Kindle e-book format. These books would soon be available as mobile apps on Apple iOS and Android devices. Shobha is a software professional with over 25 years' experience in embedded software development.
www.themathsclinic.co.uk

Printed in Great Britain
by Amazon

49463090R00052